What people are s
Trumpet According to

"Lately I have been reading this interesting book *Trumpet According to Dennis Najoom,* based on his experiences and knowledge. Very good concepts. Highly recommended. Good job Dennis."

—Esteban Batallán, Principal Trumpet, Chicago Symphony Orchestra

"Últimamente he estado leyendo este interesante libro *Trumpet According to Dennis Najoom*, basado en sus experiencias y conocimientos. Muy buenos conceptos. Muy recomendado. Buen trabajo Dennis."

—Esteban Batallán, Trompeta Principal, Orquestra Sinfónica de Chicago

"I've been reading through your most excellent trumpet book *Trumpet According to Dennis Najoom,* and want to congratulate you for writing such a fine book...It's more than a trumpet book. I am very impressed by the quality of your insights, and also the wisdom from your experience in orchestras... I peruse it often. This book should be read by many trumpet players, and I'll buy a couple to give as gifts...Kudos for your writing! Good exercises in there too!!!"

—Ed Hoffman, Retired Associate Principal Trumpet, Baltimore Symphony Orchestra, Faculty of Peabody Conservatory of Music

"I have a new go to pocket book of trumpet advice to give to my students and to rave about to my friends. Thank you for your invaluable contribution to trumpet pedagogy."

—Mike Zonshine, Former Principal Trumpet, Honolulu Symphony Orchestra, L.A. Freelancer, Trumpet faculty at California State Polytechnic University Pomona, Colburn Community School.

"Got mine today - every trumpet player should own this. Wit, wisdom, and uncommonly direct common sense, *Trumpet According to Dennis Najoom,* is a superb addition to our literature from one of our finest players and colleagues - thank you, Dennis!"

—Hank Mautner, Retired Professor of trumpet, freelance trumpet player and soloist with the Blue Wisp Big Band

Trumpet
According to Dennis Najoom

or

Techniques for Enhancing Your Playing

By Dennis Najoom

Cover design, book design, and all photography by Jennifer Najoom
Photographic illustrations with ToonCamera App by HELLOTOON,INC
Music design with Harry Abramowitz
Non-photo illustrations courtesy of Pixabay.com

Trumpet According to Dennis Najoom
Techniques for Enhancing Your Playing

ISBN:978-1-7359979-0-2

Acknowledgements

I would like to thank my wife Jenny, my daughter Anna and her husband Kiljoong, and grandson Walden, for their love and support. I learn from them every day. I'd also like to thank my mother Evelyn for teaching me about music and music theory since before I can remember. My Uncle George Fulginiti, my first trumpet teacher, and all my teachers, students, and colleagues. I have learned more from you than you have learned from me.

I would like to thank The Milwaukee Symphony Orchestra for letting me be a full time member for 43 years, and all the members and subs of the trumpet section and entire brass section for their superb musicianship, professionalism and friendship. I would also like to give great thanks to the members of my band, The Little Lake Stompers: Bill Helmers, Kirk Ferguson, Lou Cucunato, Glen Quarrie, Paul Westfahl, Scott Tisdel, and Derek Volkman, for exploring and helping me learn a variety of musical styles.

I would also like to thank Marvin Stamm for his friendship, support and helping to bring back my love of performing music. I also owe thanks to Doc Severinsen for all the years of mentor-ship as Pops Conductor of The Milwaukee Symphony Orchestra, whether he knew it or not.

Thank you to Harry Abramowiz and Murray Gordon for your encouragement and help with the editing. Finally, Jenny, thank you again for the endless hours spent over three years formatting, editing, and improving this book in every way. You caught so many questionable and unclear sections, and held my feet to the fire.

Thank You!

CONTENTS

Preface

A Picture of Musicianship

Picture two vases. Both are perfectly made in every way. One is plain and one has beautiful art etched on it.

One is an example of absolute perfection of craftsmanship. You can re-create identical ones that are perfect in every detail. However, if it should get a nick or chip in it, it becomes worthless and a sore sight. It's all your eye can see. You go out and buy another one.

The other is just as well made but with a difference. It has beautifully etched freehand artwork, which takes it to another level. This one also gets a chip, but the chip doesn't bother you or distract from the vase's beauty because it's a one-of-a-kind work. It's the only one that exists.

Music performance is the same.

Just think about this.

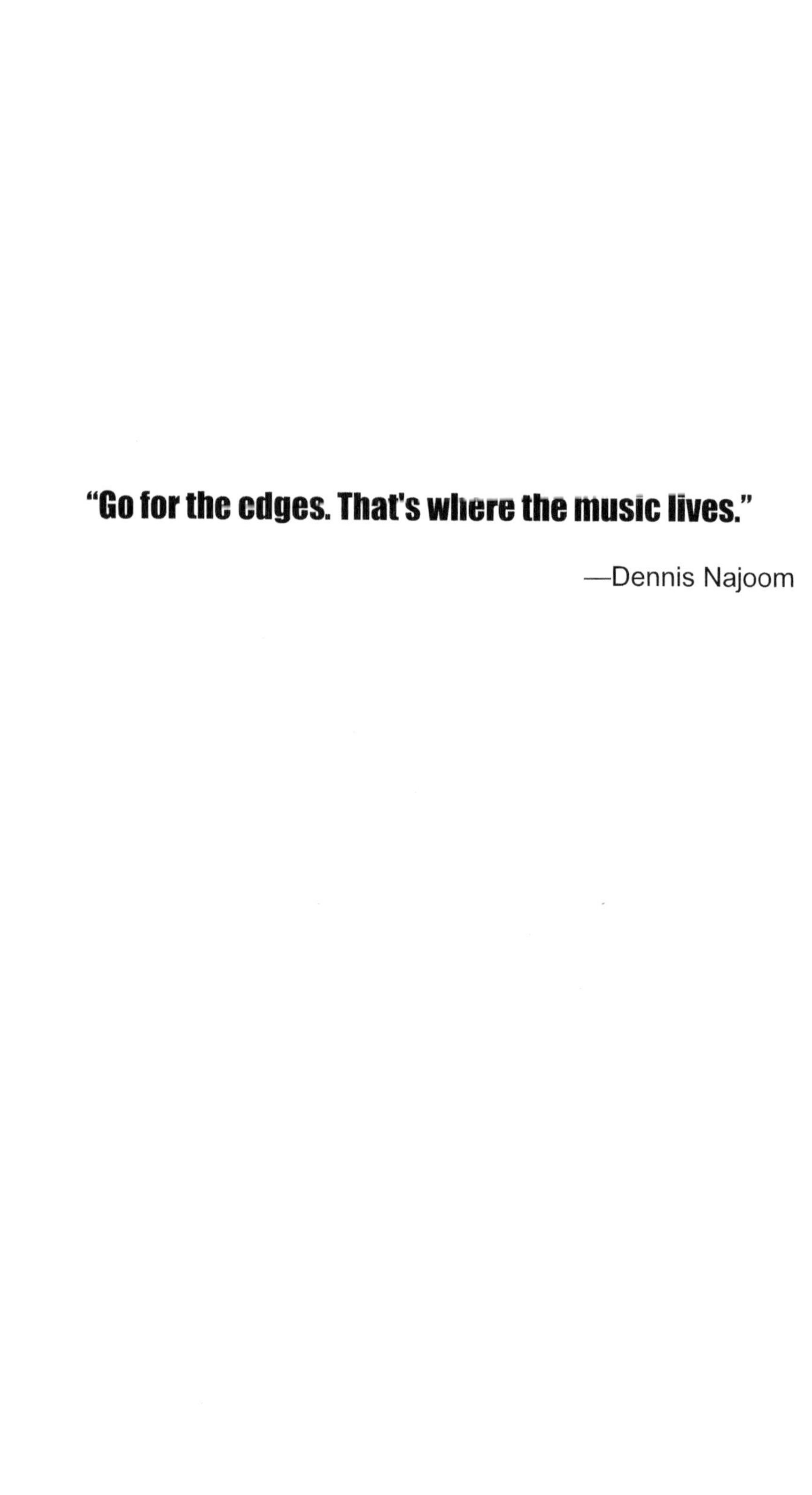

"Go for the edges. That's where the music lives."

—Dennis Najoom

Chapter 1

For Trumpet Players
and
Other Assorted Brass Players

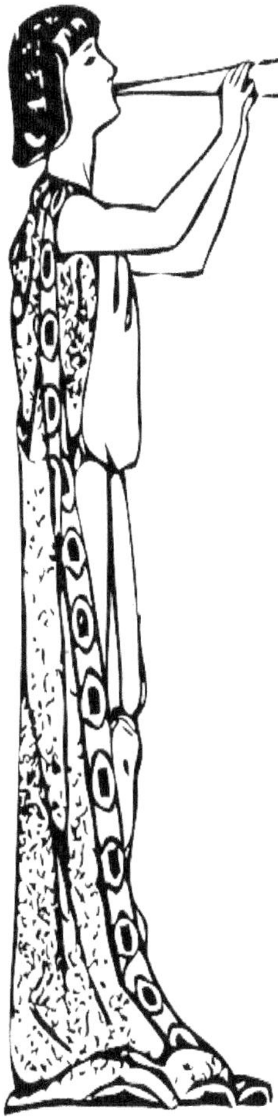

"We are all different with different physical attributes. One method does not fit all."

Caution! Read at your own risk. If you don't want to think about mechanics, don't read this book or just skip over the sections you prefer not to think about.

I suggest approaching this book by looking through it first, and then working on and exploring one section at a time. These techniques and thoughts have worked well for me and my students, but I try to tailor my teaching to each individual. I tell my students that it is quite possible that I might tell another student the opposite of what we just worked on. Just a simple example; some are too tight, and some are too loose. It's usually never this simple.

Teachers

If you are studying with a well qualified teacher and what you are being taught is different or even the opposite of what is in this book, listen to your teacher. Taking lessons with a well qualified teacher with a good track record is best. We are all different with different physical attributes. One method does not fit all.

Even the finest trumpet players in the world are searching for answers and learning from others. If there are professional teacher/performers nearby, again, who have a good track record, try to get lessons with each, but it is probably best to do it after reaching a fairly high level of proficiency. Although some of the best choose not to be in the spotlight, they, regardless of position, will be able to give you invaluable information. Don't miss out on this wealth of knowledge!

Experiment and Observe

Remember, for anything I suggest in this book, there will be fine players who may recommend the opposite. Experiment and observe, and decide what works best for you. Respect your own judgment. Lack of self-respect can be one of your biggest impediments to substantial improvement. You are the first and only person to be you, so bring us something good and original.

Musicians are Magicians

I hope this book will demystify some aspects of trumpet performance, but musicians are also magicians. It's hard to know what they're doing just by listening to them.

“Warning! Books happen when you spend three weeks in a cottage in Door County without internet.”

Dennis Najoom

Chapter 2

Warm Up Is Good

"Don't think of warm up as practice. Just think of warm up as a time to get things going without harm."

My thoughts and goals for warming up are to be consistent and play my best when it's time to perform. However, sometimes you have to be somewhat inconsistent with how you warm up. I know that I feel differently after a very hard day of playing as opposed to how I feel after a very light day or a day of no playing. Try to figure out the best course of action so you can perform your best when you need to that day. Everything you do throughout your warm up and eventual practice should have a beneficial effect upon the next time you play.

First, test your chops to determine how they feel by playing a few notes and maybe a half a scale on the mouthpiece only. This can tell you quite a bit and give you an indication as to how to proceed with your warm up.

See *Mouthpiece 1 and 2* in Appendix I at the back of this book for some of my favorite mouthpiece warm up exercises.

Don't think of warm up as practice. Just think of warm up as a time to get things going without harm. Sometimes the best thing to do is to put down the horn and come back a while later depending how beat or fresh your chops feel. If after 20 minutes or so of rest your chops feel somewhat better, play a couple of half scales and a few easy notes first on the mouthpiece and then on the trumpet. Hold the last note of them a bit to stabilize the embouchure. Rest a short time, then play a full octave scale using the *Sensitivity 1* exercises found in Appendix II at the back of this book.

Try the following exercise as a prelude to the *Sensitivity 1* and *Sensitivity 2* thought processes. Use the trumpet first, then switch to the mouthpiece playing perfectly in tune, then back to the trumpet. Now play *Sensitivity 1*.

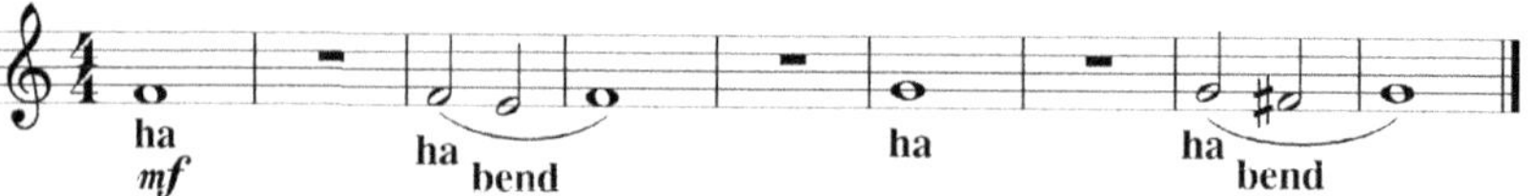

Sensitivity 1 (see Appendix II-1)

The purpose of *Sensitivity 1* is to:

- Condition your lips to respond to a whisper of air.
- Increase efficiency.
- Get you moving up and down without harm.

When going up, the resistance increases and will automatically make you get softer. Let it. As you go down the resistance will release, so go with it and allow yourself to get louder and return to the same dynamic you had when you started.

This would be a good time to take a 15 to 20 minute break. I often find, as have many of my students, that when I come back after this break I feel almost all warmed up. It's very cool when it happens.

As your chops get more and more sensitive, continue to go higher and higher and expand in both directions so that your high F above high C is as easy as your first space F.

Get More Extensive

Now, I start a more extensive warm up with plenty of rest in-between. Whatever I do I want it to feel good. Do not hurt yourself or overplay yet. Sometimes you can and sometimes you can't. Judgment call here. The point is to get your chops going gradually without injury, and each time you play after resting you are better. You should strive for a system where everything you play has a positive effect so that all aspects of your playing will get better and better throughout the day. Remember that every time you play you want it to be beneficial. In other words, some days you have to be very careful when starting your warm up, and some days you may need little or no warm up to play your best.

Note: I have noticed that players with more irregular teeth may have to take more time warming up so as to prevent injury and to get the lip to vibrate evenly.

Sensitivity 2 (see Appendix II-3)

Once you are warmed up and comfortable with *Sensitivity 1*, add *Sensitivity 2* to your normal practicing and notice how you can sense the resistance, and how easy and balanced this exercise can be. The point is, when doing *Sensitivity 2*, as you go up you will have to blow harder, or with more strength, since the back pressure will increase as you go higher. So...

- Blow with the force needed to meet the resistance.
- Don't let the increasing resistance win or in other words, make you get softer at any point as you go up.
- In this exercise, always meet the resistance as it increases.

This is the opposite of *Sensitivity 1* where you sense the resistance increasing and you let it cause you to get softer.

Once you learn to feel the resistance, it becomes easier to play the different keyed trumpets because each has different characteristics and resistance.

In Conclusion

There are many types of warm up methods to explore so experiment and observe. My favorites are:

- The *Sensitivity 1*, *Sensitivity 2* exercises in the back of this book in Appendix II.
- Easy mouthpiece buzzing.
- Exercises from the James Stamp warm up books.
- Some etudes from *Technical Studies for the Cornet* by H L Clark.

I also recommend the use of the BERP™, a buzzing and resistance tool developed by one of our finest performers and educators of the trumpet, Mario Guarneri. When Mario speaks, be sure to listen.

Your own exercises:

Chapter 3

Practicing

"Find a way to love it."

Practicing is a very individual experience, and in your early years is guided by your teacher. However, if I must write a chapter about practicing, here goes.

Basics

1. Practice slowly and in the same manor you would be playing if you were playing in the proper tempo.

2. Go through the stuff you're good at and polish it.

3. Work on the stuff you're not.

4. Listen carefully to yourself.

5. Listen carefully to your teacher.

6. Work with your teacher.

7. Come up with your own exercises and tunes without any music.

Getting Out of a Rut

We all get into a rut sometimes, here are some ideas to get out.

- Try practicing the loud excerpts softer, around an mp.
- Try practicing the soft excerpts louder, around an mf.
- When working on the piccolo, try to practice as softly as you can as you go up.

This kind of practice can help break through some problems you may have and get you unstuck and out of a rut. Besides, you never know what you might be asked to do by the Maestro.

Play Without Music

Play without music a lot! It's great for everything. I don't mean memorizing the music, just play stuff there is no music for, like a jazz musician improvising. The great Stan Getz said something that pertains to all musical styles, *"I would play if nobody listened to it. Any jazz musician, if there's nobody around to listen, would play for the sheer joy of improvising music."*

The best medicine for improving is to love practicing. Find a way to love it.

Chapter 4

The Sweet Spot

To know it is to love it.

The sweet spot is quite often referred to as the slot, core, center, etc., but my preferred term is "sweet spot". Maybe this is because I have been known to hack up some golf courses and very rarely will I hit a shot so perfectly I don't even feel the contact with the ball as it soars beautifully. When this happens I know that I've hit the sweet spot.

Playing in the sweet spot or near the sweet spot is most desirable. When playing in the sweet spot:

- Our tone is the most resonant.
- Our tone contains the full spectrum of overtones.
- Our playing is most efficient.

How to do it? I will suggest what works for me, however, I'm sure there are many other fine and effective approaches described by numerous others.

Where is the beautiful sweet spot?

It's near the top of the note, just under the area of the note that really sounds stuffy and like a bad vacuum cleaner. There is very little room to the upside so you only venture there to raise the intonation a bit. If you are playing above the sweet spot not only will you sound bad, but you won't be able to raise the pitch, and you will also have to pull the tuning slide out further which doesn't do much to help the playing characteristics of the trumpet.

Think of a note as a vertical oval and not a circle, with the sweet spot about a quarter of the way down.

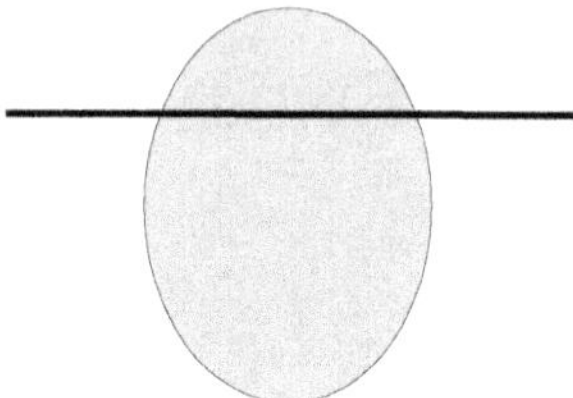

This is just a rough approximation. Your ear is your guide. Bending down past the sweet spot is at least as disgusting as going up, and as you continue down it keeps getting worse. I'm getting sick just thinking about it.

How do you find the beautiful sweet spot?

First, remember that you can bend a note much further down than you can go up. Here are two ways:

Way One

1. Play a second line G.
2. Bend it down into the disgusting sound then slowly bring it up to the beautiful, full, resonant, effortless, sweet spot.
3. Pass upward into the disgusting vacuum cleaner sound, then back down to the beautiful sweet spot.

Your ear and your musical taste is your guide. Once you have found it, look at the tuner then look at your tuning slide to see where it is. If flat push in, if sharp pull out. Keep repeating this process until your tuning slide lines up with the sweet spot so you don't have to adjust much one way or the other while playing. *Danger!! Do not look at the tuner while you are searching for the sweet spot.*

Way Two

1. Play a second line G on the trumpet for about 4 seconds.
2. Play the G on the mouthpiece perfectly in tune for about the same amount of time,
3. Then quickly play the G back on the trumpet.

This simple exercise can tell you a lot. Quite often when you play on the mouthpiece it will initially be out of tune or even a different note. Repeat this series a couple of times then:

4. Play F, G, A, Bb, up and down slurred, and as smoothly as possible.
5. Play the same phrase on the mouthpiece.
6. Go back to the trumpet quickly and play it again.

Use this technique on other musical passages you encounter to help improve the passage. The better you can play the passage on the mouthpiece in tune, the easier the passage becomes and the more efficient your chops become.

Chapter 5

Articulation
The Beginning of Sound

"The Attack"

The beginning of sound is sometimes called the *attack*. An interesting word for starting a note, 'attack'. Some other ways of describing the beginning of the note could be; '*release of the air*', '*beginning of the buzz*', '*the start of vibration*', '*beginning of sound*', or perhaps just '*tongue release*'.

Starting The Note

When we start a note we release the air at some speed. A nice exercise is to go back-and-forth between an air beginning or *breath start,* and a tongued beginning or *tongue release*. Keep the tone the same on the tongued beginning as on the air beginning. I like to start the air beginning with the syllable 'ha'. Go back and forth "ha ta ha ta" etc. Now try controlling the speed of the air by blowing without the trumpet at different speeds, with and without tightening your abdominal muscles. Observe.

A Note Has Three Parts

In practical applications, think of each note as having three parts; a beginning, middle, and end, each having the same or different volumes, and for different amounts of time. For example, an orchestral *marcato sostenuto* will have a slightly longer first part of the note than a *sforzando piano* would have and, the *sforzando piano* would quickly diminuendo to nothing where the *marcato sostenuto* would sustain. When you think about this technique there is no limit to how much you can adjust the note.

Here are some picture examples:

The boxes above represent a generic note with no markings on it. You play the beginning, the middle and the end of each note the same volume.

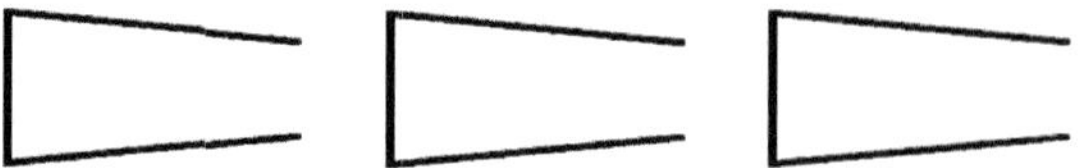

The figures above represent a note that is started by the tongue and gradually gets a little softer.

The figures above represent a note that swells in the middle part of the note. Generally, this technique is not recommended for good ensemble playing.

The figures above represent a note that begins strong, diminuendos slightly, stays steady, then ends tapered slightly to prevent an abrupt ending. Depending upon tempo, you might try thinking that the first, loudest part lasts for a 16th note, then becomes slightly softer with no diminuendo, finishing with an open ending as opposed to an abrupt ending. Try this at about ♩ = 80.

The figure above represents a *marcato sostenuto* technique. It is similar to the previous example, except these notes are connected without break. The only reason why one note ends is because you have started the next.

This last technique is controlled by your tongue using a constant even air stream stopped and started by the tongue, keeping the same air pressure from the beginning to the end of each note. This takes quite a bit of practice. This technique can be used for playing extremely short notes very loudly with spaces in between. Of course it can be done softly as well. The end of the note can also be tapered slightly so you do not hear an abrupt ending... lots of practice needed. Be very careful when using this technique. I found it works well in pieces like Stravinsky's "Firebird Infernal Dance". I was taught this by Armando Ghitalla when I was working on the "Firebird". The effortless power you can generate with this technique is quite amazing. You can also ruin pieces if this technique is used incorrectly and inappropriately. Use extreme caution!

Practicing Articulation

Practice articulation with a variety of beginnings keeping all notes attached and at various tempos. Go from the smoothest legato to the hardest marcato on one note while keeping all notes attached. Do not get shorter as you play more marcato. Try using this technique going up and down scales. Observe. Now, use different rhythms and make up your own exercises. Get away from the page. *Use your ear.* Use the same technique with double and triple tonguing. Remember to keep your best long tone quality when you go into double and triple tonguing from single tonguing.

When single tonguing short notes, as you go faster and faster there is a point where the notes must reconnect. You may be asked to play short and fast by a conductor but at this point the only control you have is the shape of the note and how far you diminuendo.

Tongue Placement

Where do you aim your tongue when you begin the note? It depends on where *you* get the best sound and most efficiency. Think of your top teeth as a target. Try releasing the air at different points behind the top teeth from high to low and low to high, but do not go below the top teeth to articulate. You should be able to find the best spot to articulate using this technique. It's quite amazing how this procedure affects ease of production and efficiency. Experiment and observe.

One of my favorite things to practice is starting a note with a breath beginning, then a note with a tongue release while keeping all the notes attached:

HaaaTahaaaHaaaTahaaa, etc.

Then with a separation:

Haa......Tahaa......Haa.....Tahaa

Keep the same quality of sound with the tongue release as with the breath release. When starting the sound with this breath start technique, do it without a pop at the beginning of the note.

Add these techniques to your tool box. The successful professional has many many tools in the toolbox. The only limit is your imagination.

Chapter 6

Embouchure Operation
or
Aperture Control

"It's all about the balance between the aperture and air."

Keep the center relaxed with firm corners. How firm? This is the billion dollar question.

Placement

The placement of the mouthpiece varies depending on your dental and physical structure. You have to find the best spot for you. Quite often the mouthpiece will naturally find where the buzz ring should be, and trying to force it to be precisely in the center can prevent you from finding the best spot for it. I like to think; Mouthpiece, Lip, Teeth. Bring the mouthpiece to the lip and then to the teeth using only the amount of pressure needed.

Aperture

The opening and closing of the aperture is mostly controlled by simply moving your chin up and down. You can't control the aperture very much without moving the jaw and distorting the embouchure. The aperture does open and close as you play up and down but only very slightly. Some say the secret to playing in the high register is to be able to develop an extremely small aperture. Doc Severinsen describes how playing in the high register is like squeezing a water hose tighter and tighter so the stream goes further and further and becomes more intense.

Three Ways to Play

Here are three ways to train your aperture. If you can do this as described, you are playing correctly. You may think differently or not think at all about how you are doing these exercises, but all that matters is that they come out right. *See Appendix III to see these exercises written out.*

1. Play a scale and a half from low C to G above the staff up and down at the same dynamic level. Listen and observe what is necessary to accomplish this exercise so the quality of the sound stays the same.
2. Play the same scale starting very loudly, and go up evenly to an extreme pianissimo, and back down with a mirror image crescendo. Observe.
3. For me, this one is the most fun and interesting. Play the same scale up and down, but this time start as softly as you can and make an extreme crescendo up to the top and mirror image it back down. If you do this exercise properly it will be the only time your aperture can remain constant without closing on the way up and reopening on the way down.

Of course it is obvious that from extreme forte to extreme pianissimo your aperture will be the most active. Get rid of the thought that when you go higher you will always have to use more air. It's the proper balance between air and aperture that creates the most efficiency. If you try to use more air from loud to soft going up you'll just start getting louder, out of balance, and won't be able to do an even diminuendo going up.

Air and Aperture Balance

Keep in mind that it is always the air and aperture balance for which we strive. It's all about the balance between the aperture and air. I like to refer to it as the air/aperture formula. Your ear and your musical taste is your ultimate guide regardless of how you approach playing. As a great musician once said, *"If it sounds good, it is good."* Come up with your own exercises. It's fun and breaks you away from always looking at the page and frees your ear to hear better.

Notice that in the 'Three Ways to Play' section you are focusing on dynamics, aperture, and air. When doing the Sensitivity Studies in Appendix I, you are focusing on resistance or the feeling of back pressure. These are different mind games to play.

Corner Firmness

A great orchestral trumpet icon taught me the puffing cheeks exercise described below as a means to help establish the embouchure. The other stuff you can blame on me.

The Puffing Cheek Exercise

A good starting point is second line G. I like to think of this note as the neutral zone note from where you go up and go down.

1. Play a second line G in the sweet spot around a comfortable mf, no louder, then gradually puff your cheeks and keep the same sound and pitch. Observe where the note wants to go.

2. Once you have a beautiful relaxed sound with absolutely no stress in the tone, gradually bring your cheeks back and slowly firm the corners until the pitch starts to rise. Once it rises, relax back to where it was just be-

fore the pitch raised. That is how firm the corners should be on the G.

3. From second line G, as you go up the corners can firm, and as you go down the corners can firm, but keep the same quality of sound in each direction. Relax the buzzing area and firm the corners to taste but don't let your lips go in as you go higher and higher.

Note: There are many other methods and ideas about embouchure development and operation. Be open to them as well.

Endurance

One very important key to building endurance is being able to practice a lot without injuring your chops. Chops, just like all other muscles, have to be strengthened methodically. Strength, sensitivity, and playing in the 'sweet spot' is the goal. Once you have injured your chops you have to heal. Not playing, and playing very lightly, can help bring them back.

Chapter 7

Breathing

for Trumpet Playing Purposes

"The more tools you have, the better the chance you will survive."

So much has been said and written about how to take a breath for trumpet playing purposes it takes my breath away. So I'll add my two cents and give a few simple suggestions you can fool around with.

I'll start with a concept that I don't understand.

The Wide Open Mouth Technique

For this method you open your mouth wide to take a breath before playing. Try opening your mouth wide open and take a breath. Then, what one has to do after the wide open or 'Oh' breath is to reset your embouchure in order to play.

Next are some concepts that I do like:

The Same Syllable Technique

I find it much more efficient to breathe in using the same syllable I'm going to use when starting the given note. Such as Hahh in, and Tahh out. Hahh -Tahh. The use of syllables is a personal thing. Try Tuh, Tee, Too, Tih, etc., or just simply release the air. But it's important to have the sound in mind that you want to produce.

Here is a fun exercise to try: Take in air at different speeds using different oral openings.

Breathe and Relax

Just take a deep breath into a relaxed body, and then play what is appropriate. Sit in a comfortable but upright position and keep your body soft, fill with air and observe how it feels. Try to keep this feeling as you play and not collapse your gut.

To experience a full relaxed breath suck in air slowly through a small circular opening between your lips and observe how your body reacts. Make sure you are sitting in an upright position with no muscles engaged. Imagine filling up a balloon as you breathe in.

80 – 20 Breathing

Another way to breath before playing that often comes in handy is to take in about 80% of your full breath, then top it off with the last 20% just before playing. If you have to wait to come in after that first 80%, make sure you keep open and not use the glottal stop. We used to have a conductor who would sometimes give the downbeat before he even got back to the podium for an encore. We survived by taking the 80% breath well in advance so we would be ready for the quick downbeat and only have to take a quick 20% breath on top. The 20% on top also breaks any tension that may have built. Rick Metzger, former principal trumpet of the Milwaukee Symphony Orchestra taught me this.

Remember it takes a bit of time to take a good relaxed breath, so don't try to take it during the last eighth note or 16th note of a fast tempo before playing. Plan in the previous measure where and when to take the breath. Try the Pre-planned Breathing exercise in the next section.

Pre-planned Breathing Exercise

A good exercise is to start with two 4/4 bars. (See the exercise below.) You begin your breath in the first bar and play on the first beat of the second bar. For each step you'll have to take a faster breath, but <u>make sure you remain relaxed and have the same feeling you did at the end of your first breath.</u>

1. Take a breath on the first beat and continue breathing in until it's time to play on the first beat of the next measure.
2. Then start your breath on the second beat and do the same thing.
3. Then start your breath on the third beat and do the same thing.
4. Finally, start your breath on the forth beat and do the same thing.

It's also good to practice taking a very fast breath just before coming in and still remain relaxed. From there, do whatever the music calls for, soft, loud, high, low etc.

Remember, the more tools you have the better the chance you will survive.

Chapter 8

Finger Technique & Air Stream

"The goal is to be able to play faster and faster, evenly."

Air, embouchure, fingers and tongue are what we have to work with. They are all controlled and coordinated by our brain and our musical judgment.

Air is Stupid

I like to think of the air as stupid. It has no idea what the fingers are doing. Essentially, you blow a steady stream of air while you press the valves down. When working on fast passages where all the notes are slurred, the trick is to keep the air stream constant through every note. *Technical Studies for the Cornet* by H L Clark is excellent for working on this technique. Using "Etude 2", play slowly and press the valves down firmly and quickly while keeping a perfectly even stream of air. Gradually get faster and faster. This is easier said than done but if you can achieve this your playing will become much smoother especially on fast chromatics. It will help you play Rimsky-Korsakov's *The Flight of The Bumble Bee*.

Observe Your Air Stream

One way to practice keeping your air stream constant, is to play the first note of Clark's exercise, (see above), and hold it throughout while watching the notes go by. Observe what happens to your air stream. It could change and become uneven, even if you just imagine each note in your head. Once you can hold a steady tone throughout, try to play the exercise as written and see if you can keep the air stream even.

If the passage is still uneven, <u>have some other trumpet player press down the valves while you attempt to keep a steady airstream.</u> Also, have the person press the valves randomly so you never know when the valve is going down in advance. This is the feeling you want. It most likely will feel very strange at first but try to keep this feeling when you press down the valves yourself. Imagine playing bag pipes.

Valve Changes and Tempo

Another thing to pay attention to is, keeping the valve changes that are very easy, and the ones that are more awkward and difficult the same tempo. You may have to imagine slowing down the easy valve changes and speeding up the difficult ones to keep an even tempo. As you develop, the goal is to be able to play faster and faster, evenly.

Chapter 9

Tongue Placement and Movement

Where does the tongue go?

I've often wondered if the size of the head and oral cavity has something to do with tongue placement. It seems that trumpet players with big heads promote something described as "high tongue". Maybe trumpet players with small heads already have a high enough tongue placement. We also know many trumpet players with small heads who have big heads. (Sorry)

The Back of the Tongue

The back of the tongue naturally goes up as you go up into the high register, and lowers in back as you head to the lower range. In general I don't think you have to think too much about this.

I like to think of using the syllable 'Ah' from around low C to around F# or G above the staff. Past that, go up using 'Ee'. Below low C I like 'Aw' because it gives a richer more pleasant quality. So...

- 'Aw' below low C
- 'Ah' from low C to first space above the staff G
- 'Ee' on up

The back of the tongue helps focus the air and supports aperture. Try not to over think this process. Your ear and musical taste is your ultimate guide. Don't fight it.

The Tip of the Tongue

Now where does the tip of the tongue go? Experiment with aiming your tongue at different spots behind your top teeth. Start high at the gum line and gradually tongue lower and lower on the back of the top teeth until you find the sweet spot where you get the most efficiency, energy, ease, fullness of sound and power. When searching don't go below the top teeth. Try tonguing below the top teeth just as a learning experience. Do this in different ranges. You might find that the tip always hits the same spot as you go up and down or the tongue may entirely rise as you go up and lower as you go down.

Fool around with this concept a bit but the bottom line is always *do what works the best for you*. Don't get hung up on a technique that stymies you. What comes naturally is quite often the best approach.

The Front of the Tongue

Essentially, the front of the tongue stops the the air and releases the air. That's it. Anything more gets in the way.

These are just techniques with which you can experiment, hoping that you find what is best for you. Be flexible. What's right for you can be somewhere in-between or anywhere else. Your ear and musical taste is your guide.

Chapter 10

Slurring and The Alcohol Connection

"The embouchure needs to be flexible, dynamic, and able to move quickly."

Perfect slurring is a beautiful thing. The lips should be in continuous motion supported by a steady stream of air from one note to the next. Think of a guitar player tuning the guitar string up to the desired level and not going past. The longer you hold the bottom note perfectly in tune without any telegraphing as to what is coming next, the better and smoother the slur. If done expertly you will be able to connect any interval without hearing the notes in-between.

Slurring and Baseball

The embouchure needs to be flexible, dynamic, and able to move quickly. For a baseball batter, the player has to have relaxed arms to be able to swing quickly and suddenly. If the arm muscles are flexed and tight the movement will be stiff and slow. This is the same with the golf swing or throwing a ball. Same with the chops. They have to be ready to move instantly and quickly to execute a beautiful slur.

Drunken Slurring

Slurring and The Alcohol Connection may sound absurd and it certainly can be construed that way, but if you stretch a bit you might see a connection. 'Specially after a couple a martoonies.

The point is that alcohol will cause you to slur your words up and down *with smooth connections*. Think “slowly up and slowly down”. This is a way you can practice slurring. A good example of someone who slurs after drinking too much is....Oh! I can’t say? I am not advocating imbibing in alcoholic beverages. Some of the best comedians who did drunk bits were not drunks. Try it and make believe you have had a few too many (really).

How to Practice Slurring – One Technique

It always seems like magic to me when a beautiful connected octave slur is played perfectly without hearing the notes in-between. So the question is, how does one go about practicing this? For a period of time during my career I had trouble with octave slurs, but this method worked after many years of playing and having tried different techniques. I got the job done by playing the bottom note as long as possible then playing the note an octave higher with a breath attack. It’s a valid technique but not the best way to play a smooth octave slur.

How to Practice Slurring – A Better Technique

During a difficult time I lost the ability to do a perfectly smooth slur. I had always done it intuitively, but after a while I realized that I had no idea how I was doing it. This is one of the dangers of playing purely intuitively. Eventually, I figured it out again.

Here is a practice technique that I like, and practice often. It can be learned in a matter of minutes. Let’s go for an octave slur.

1. Start going up to the top note by playing (slurring) all the notes in-between until you get to the top note. If you are going from G up to G the notes in-between are C and E. Slur up to C then to E then to G evenly over a quarter note at about 60 or slower.

2. Then gradually start the slur with all the notes later and later and closer to the top G. Keep the air constant and the lips in motion between the notes. Do not stab at the top note as you may pass it.

3. Then, slur from G to G with all the notes after the fourth sixteenth of the beat. Think; 1,2,3,4, slur. Try to keep the volume the same from bottom to top.

4. Finally, if you have slurred up the octave smoothly and quickly enough the beautiful octave slur will magically occur without hearing the notes in between.

Chapter 11

Good Intonation and Vibrato
or
Sound Like You're Playing In Tune

"Be ready to adjust for what ever the situation."

Intonation

Playing in tune involves making the best choice at any given time. This applies to other aspects of playing as well, such as style, rhythm, dynamics, etc., and is every bit as important when dealing with intonation. This chapter will help you to decide what is the best choice.

Be Sensitive and Flexible

Be sensitive to your musical surroundings. If you have preplanned the pitch you are going to use, it can be trouble for you and everyone else. Here's an example. The orchestra is playing and you're not and you have an exposed solo coming up and while you're waiting to come in, the pitch changes a bit. Your job is to hear the ambient pitch and blend with it when you come in with your solo. At the very least, change instantly and artistically once you realize things have changed.

Be flexible, not rigid, and be ready to adjust for whatever the situation, because you never really know what's coming. For example, a baseball batter keeps loose before swinging, or a boxer who must keep loose before a quick knockout punch.

Good Pitch

Good pitch is making the right choices at the right time, similarly to a jazz improviser playing the 'good notes' as they are weaving through the changes. So, maybe good pitch is like improvising because trying to plan in advance doesn't always work.

There are always exceptions to everything. Even playing out of tune one way or another can be an effective way to enhance a performance. A good example is when a fine jazz singer starts a note flat and finishes beautifully in tune.

Quality of tone can help or hinder how your pitch is perceived. You can have a bright and thin sound, or a dark and wide sound and still be in tune... but it might not sound in tune. One of the greatest orchestral trumpet players of all time (not me) was heard to say, "You want to know how to play in tune? Play with a good sound."

To find out more about producing a quality tone, see Chapter 4 "*The Sweet Spot*" which describes playing in the center, or slot.

The Tuner

Tuners have many good uses but can really mess things up if used incorrectly. Don't follow the tuner attached to your instrument. Listen and blend with the ambient pitch. Watching a tuner attached to your bell or on your stand while performing will distract you from:

- Playing musically.
- Being aware of your ensemble around you.
- Your attention to the conductor.

- Your place in the music.
- Not making mistakes.

Using a tuner while playing makes it impossible to give the music your full attention. In short, tuners can tend to screw you up. *Looking at a tuner while playing in an orchestra is like texting while driving.* Instead, listen and sound good.

Vibrato

Google defines vibrato as: "*A rapid, slight variation in pitch in singing or playing some musical instruments, producing a stronger or richer tone.*" * Vibrato can make you or break you.

Essentially, vibrato goes down from the proper pitch and returns back to the proper pitch, in other words, it goes in and out of tune. Make sure you return to the proper pitch!

How To Do It

There are many ways to produce a vibrato. Some common ways are;

- Hand: Using your hand to move the instrument back and forth horizontally instead of vertically.
- Diaphragm: Using your diaphragm to change the speed of the air with pulses.
- Whatever it is that singers do. Please don't ask me.
- Lip/Jaw: *See Below*

Lip/Jaw is what works for me. I am not an expert at the other methods so you had better ask someone else about them. Lip/Jaw involves slightly moving your jaw down and up and/or moving the pitch down and back up.

---

*Google Search. Google. 20 June 2019. Web. 20 June 2019

How to Practice It

Start at a metronome marking of around sixty beats per minute. First try two vibrati to the beat, then three, then four, then five, then six. I find five to the beat, with a quarter note at about 60 beats per minute, is most pleasant for orchestral playing and usually done very lightly. In some jazz ballads you may want to use a slower and deeper vibrato, down to four vibrati to a beat. Or, start with no vibrato and then add some at the end of the note. As you can see its possibilities are endless. But, be careful of when and where you use vibrato. Tread carefully and practice it.

Sometimes I move my hand back and forth in the air over the valves, just for effect. ;)

When in doubt, don't use it until the music calls to you.

Chapter 12

Transposition Made Simple

"Look up one whole step and add two sharps."

Ha Ha. Did you fall for it? This chapter demonstrates the method I find easiest to use.

For a quick transposition to learn without a detailed explanation, we'll transpose a C part using a B♭ trumpet. This is the most common transposition and is useful if you want to read a fake book in C concert or play along using a hymnal in church which is also in C concert.

☞ **Look up one whole step and add two sharps.**

Note: Sharps and flats cancel each other out. For example, if there is already one flat in the C part, you still look up one whole step but add one sharp instead of two.

Transposition Basics

Using the following approach, you can transpose from a trumpet in any key.

With the above transposition as an example, a C part using a B♭ trumpet, I'll show you how to figure it out on your own.

I ask three questions:

1.) <u>Which way</u> on the staff will you have to look? Up or down?

This has got to do with the physical size of the two instruments being compared.

- If you're using a larger instrument than the part is written for, you will look up.
- If you're using a smaller instrument than the part is written for, you will go down.

In the case of reading a C concert part on a B♭ trumpet, you will look up because a B♭ trumpet is a larger instrument than a C trumpet.

2.) <u>What is the interval</u> between the key of the instrument you are holding, and the key of the trumpet for which the music was originally written?

- Major 2nd, minor 2nd, Major 3rd etc.

In our example above; from (trumpet in) B♭ to (trumpet in) C is a Major 2nd.

3.) <u>How far up or down from concert C</u> is the interval you found in question 2?

Where you land on the staff tells you your new key and therefore how many flats or sharps to add to the key signature. With this system you can always think of it as a major key. (A minor key is just a major key that starts on a different note.)

For our example; <u>up</u> a <u>Major 2nd</u> from concert C is D Major. D Major has 2 sharps.

See the chart at the back of this chapter to determine how many sharps or flats to add to the written key signature. Sharps cancel flats and vice versa.

So, to transpose a C part for a B♭ trumpet, look up one whole step and add two sharps.

Some other examples:

- If you find that you need to go up a Minor third from C, that is an E♭. The key of E♭ Major has 3 flats, so you look up a third and add three flats. I will just look up to the next space or line and think three flats.
- Playing an F part on a C trumpet; I will still ask all three questions and determine that I have to look up a fourth and add one flat.
- Playing an F Alto part on a C trumpet; I will look down a fifth and add one flat. This is the same transposition as reading a D trumpet part on an A piccolo.
- Etc., etc., etc.

Note: Sometimes you have to account for parts written in a higher or lower octave than what is actually sounded.

This formula works for any key trumpet to any other key trumpet. There are trumpets in all keys.

Now that you understand what's going on, here's a quick way to figure out the new key.

- Small trumpet to big: Look down
- Big trumpet to small: Look up
- Find the interval between the keys of the 2 trumpets
- Look up or down this interval from concert C.

This note is your new key, a major key.

- Add the appropriate sharps or flats (see the chart at the end of this chapter.)

Make It Easier

When I look up or down I don't worry about the quality of the interval. Major 3rd or Perfect 4th or Minor 3rd etc. I just change the key in my head and look up or down so many lines or so many spaces. There are times, however, when it gets complicated, such as in "Don Juan" by R. Strauss where knowing the quality of the interval is helpful.

I'll admit to putting in a fingering under the note occasionally. When you are performing no one can see your part. They can only hear you.

Tips

- 'Trumpet in F Alto' is the same transposition on a C trumpet as 'Trumpet in D' is on an A piccolo trumpet. Both down a 5th with 1 flat added.
- By the way, play the Haydn and Hummel Concertos on an E♭ trumpet unless you are Robert Nagel or Rafael Mendez. The Hummel is sometimes played on an E trumpet in the key of E. Armando Ghitalla recorded the Hummel in E on a Martin C trumpet. It is a truly amazing recording*.
- Sometimes it's simpler to use enharmonic equivalents to make a passage easier to read, for example thinking F# instead of G♭.
- What helped me to get better at transposition was to practice Orchestral Excerpts. You get your transposition work in but also technique practice and you learn the orchestral repertoire. Beautiful!

**Armando Ghitalla Trumpet,* Pierre Monteux conductor, Wellesley MA, Cambridge Records, Library Of Congress Cat. #: R64-1683, Stereo LP

If you still need help, find a local professional who understands orchestral trumpet performance. ***Note:*** People with different instruments may use different methods for transposing, so learn from an orchestral trumpet player if your goal is to play in an orchestra.

Quick Guide to Transposition

When it is 5:00am and you're playing an Easter or Christmas gig, or was out too late after a concert and had a few, sometimes the brain doesn't want to figure out a transposition. So, here is a quick guide to relieve brain fog. Copy the next page, put it in all your cases, have a couple coffees and make sure you have the applicable trumpet in hand. Just don't sell this, okay?

Dennis Najoom's Quick Guide to Transposition

Going **Up** ↑

Half Step	Add 7 sharps. - or - Look up a step and add 5 flats.
Whole Step	Look up a step and add 2 sharps.
Minor 3rd	Look up a third and add 3 flats.
Major 3rd	Look up a third and add 4 sharps.
Perfect 4th	Look up a fourth and add 1 flat.
Tri-tone	Look up a fourth and add 6 sharps. - or - Look up a fifth and add 6 flats
Perfect 5th	Look up a fifth and add 1 sharp.

Going **Down** ↓

Half Step	Add 7 flats. - or - Look down a step and add 5 sharps.
Whole Step	Look down a step and add 2 flats.
Minor 3rd	Look down a third and add 3 sharps.
Major 3rd	Look down a third and add 4 flats.
Perfect 4th	Look down a fourth and add 1 sharp.
Tri-tone	Look down a fourth and add 6 flats. - or - Look down a fifth and add 6 sharps. - or - Write it out. - or - Use a different trumpet.
Perfect 5th	Look down a fifth and add 1 flat.

Chapter 13

Mouthpiece Selection

"Does this mouthpiece make me happy?"

The selection of the right mouthpiece is a very personal thing and can be confusing given the many choices out there today, so I can't recommend any specific mouthpiece. It really depends upon what kind of playing you do, your inherent tone, and physical abilities.

Some say to play the smallest mouthpiece you can and some say to play the largest mouthpiece you can. It's quite possible you could end up with the same size mouthpiece. Being flexible is very important given the wide range of playing a trumpet player will encounter.

Find Your Mouthpiece

What do you look for when trying out a new mouthpiece? These are the questions I like to ask when considering a mouthpiece.

Ask yourself;

- *Does this mouthpiece make me happy?*
- *Does it make me want to play?*
- *Does it encourage musicality?*
- *Is it comfortable enough?*

What is important for the kind of playing you do?

- *How's my articulation?*
- *How's my flexibility?*
- *How's my sound?*
- *Does it make it easier to play what I usually play?*

And ultimately;

- *Does it make me play better?*

What is the Equipment?

There is no shame in going to your gig or rehearsal with five different mouthpieces and a few different trumpets, at least that's what I tell myself. I usually travel with an extremely deep flugelhorn type fitted to go into a trumpet receiver, and ones that get consecutively shallower. I rarely change rims. I find that I'm not very good at going from a small diameter rim to a larger diameter rim back and forth in the orchestra. I find it best to keep the same rim even on piccolo trumpet during concerts that require both piccolo trumpet and larger trumpets. If I were preparing for a piccolo recital or Bach's Brandenburg Concerto No. 2, I would go to a smaller diameter. Again, this is very personal.

In general, I have used a variety of excellent mouthpieces including mouthpieces made for me by GR Mouthpieces and Jim New. All I can tell you is what works for me. You might need a different system.

What is the Venue?

The venue can also effect what equipment you choose to use. You may perform anywhere from the most beautiful concert hall to the deadest most horrible auditorium or gymnasium. I think I actually played in the worst one. It shall remain nameless. Thus the reason for the five mouthpieces.

Tip: It is good to play for others whom you respect, to fine tune once you get close, but only you can make your final decision on a mouthpiece.

One of my Hummus Recipes

Put in a food processor:

1 large can chickpeas drained and rinsed,
minus a few for garnish
juice of 1 lemon
1 blob of tahini
a little bit of olive oil
a little garlic
a little cumin (optional)
a little cayenne (optional)

Process until smooth. Add a little water to make it the consistency you want.

Add salt and pepper to taste and correct the seasonings.

To serve:

Pour Hummus onto a plate.
Drizzle with a little olive oil.
Garnish with parsley and reserved chickpeas.

Use pita chips or pita bread to scoop up and into mouth. Cucumbers are good too.

Chapter 14

Orchestral Pops

"Look good and play good."

Pops performance has become a mainstay for most professional orchestras and needs to be taken seriously. Orchestras need all the help they can get to survive, so it is imperative to "look good and play good".

Orchestral players need to take these Pops concerts seriously and make sure they do not come off as if these concerts are beneath them. You have a job and are getting paid. If you don't want to give it 100%, don't take the gig, and if you have a permanent gig remember that this is what being a professional is all about. Pops programming can help the organization survive. Play the Gig! Frowns, bad posture and condescending attitude will only disturb the audience, the donors, and guest performers. Be as cool as you can.

How to Approach Jazz

from an orchestral point of view

Approach jazz rhythms more idiomatically than you would with a purely classical approach. The jazz rhythms need to be stylized and interpreted rather than played strictly, but still with stylized uniformity and precision for good ensemble.

When you are swinging the dotted eighth and sixteenth, do not play the dotted eighth note short unless you're doing a Lawrence Welk retrospective show. Depending on the style, you might just accent the upbeat a bit on even eighth notes. The best thing you can do is to listen to various jazz artists and legendary big bands.

If you have to play lead or pretty high parts in the jazz idiom, don't be afraid to put away your bored out #1 mouthpiece. You might be able to play the parts, but it won't sound right and you'll have to work harder than necessary. Find a setup that will give you the sound needed with appropriate brilliance in the upper register. For much of the time when I was Pops Principal, I used my #1 and 1C screw rims and fit different depth and shaped cups and backbores to it, and also changed trumpets occasionally. The #1 rim I used is pre-1X from the early 1970s. The 1X is the closest to the #1 of long ago. Today the #1 mouthpiece is very different and much larger. Finding the best equipment can be costly and time consuming but well worth the effort.

Bring someone in

I would like to caution that for a successful Pops performance it is important to bring in a seasoned lead trumpet player who can fit into the orchestra. Not too many can do this. You can't just bring in any player with a good high range. This can be big big trouble. I mean no disrespect to these many excellent trumpet players but It is a fine and specialized art to be able to play lead trumpet in a symphony orchestra. The best can balance well within the context of the symphony orchestra and understand many different pop and jazz styles (e.g., the difference between Basie, Kenton, Harry James etc.) It's a tough job. To perform with a great lead player is a thrill and an educational experience, so embrace and enjoy the ride.

Also, if you have a guest lead trumpet player, at least bring a B-flat trumpet, if only for show, but use it if you can, and absolutely follow their lead in style, note lengths, dynamics etc.

Jazz Solos

If you have to play a Jazz style solo in the orchestra and are not used to playing in a Jazz style, go easy and don't do too much. Play it safe and don't sound like a drunken clown -- no disrespect to clowns intended! Unless you are really good at improvising, write it out or call in the local jazz expert. They will be happy to get the call and the performance will benefit.

See Appendix IV for some helpful pentatonic exercises that will help you to sound like you are playing jazz.

Tips to Help Survive the Big Band Setting within the Orchestra.

Vibrato can make you or break you in any style. For the most part don't use vibrato, especially if you are playing within the section. If you are playing a solo you might try a slower vibrato or start without vibrato on a long note then carefully add some. Listen to Chet Baker.

Learn to do a Shake. Play the lower starting note on the high side and shake the horn lightly back and forth while increasing air speed. Try not to hurt your chops. You might also try working on a slower lip trill. Listen to how the great big band players do the shake.

Practice some different syllables such as: "Du", "Dot", "Dut", "Dit", "Daah", "Daht", very short "Da" or "Duh". Listen to some of the great big bands. An excellent example is "Li'l Darlin'" by the Count Basie Band. Every big band has its own style so it would take a lifetime to learn the subtleties of each. Just try to get into the ball park.

Learn the basic blues progression and practice improvising over it. When playing the twelve-bar blues, think four bars of question, four bars of question, and four bars of answer. This can really come in handy. Forget Coltrane's "Giant Steps" for now.

Listen and play along with the great jazz artists. Streaming, LPs, CDs, or whatever is the latest, there are many fine resources for this kind of practice.

These tips are a very basic but manageable starting point. Don't shy away from embracing this style as it can help your overall musicianship and playing. Embrace and enjoy.

As the great Thelonious Monk said, "If you want to dig, you got to dig, you dig?"

Chapter 15

Orchestral Trumpet Self Management & Survival Tactics

"Be respectful of all your colleagues."

As an orchestral trumpet player we have the duty to uphold the finest practices and principles of our proud heritage.

Seriously.

First and foremost, be respectful and kind to the members of your trumpet section.

Play assertively at the right times and blend when it's required. If you are playing a part other than the first trumpet part make sure you always defer to the first trumpet player. You may not agree but it is your job to make the first trumpet player and the section sound as good as possible.

If you are the first trumpet player you have a responsibility to make sure the other players can help you sound good. Make sure you don't play so high in the upper register that it makes it very difficult for the other trumpet players to come up to you. Remember it's a team effort and not just a glorification of the principal.

Dealing with Conductors

When the conductor asks you to do something or change how

you are playing a passage, be pleasant and respectful. Nod your head and smile.

Whatever the conductor asks you to do, make sure you make it sound good in spite of what you may have been asked to do. Remember, you are the trumpet expert.

When the conductor looks at you while are you are playing, make sure you look back and hold his or her stare until they finally give up. This is a survival tactic.

Another survival tactic is to make the conductor think that you may pounce at any moment. Of course you will not do this, but they have to think you will. :)

Important

Be respectful of all your other colleagues in the orchestra and don't aim your instrument at their heads if it all possible, unless it's the trombone section of course.

Don't wear perfume or cologne, or eat an all bean dinner before the rehearsal or concert. Seriously.

Most of all, enjoy and play with joy!!

Chapter 16

Don't Rush the Return

Tips For Older and Comeback Trumpet Players

"...slow, gradual recovery is the fastest way..."

If you are anything like me, you have forgotten some of the techniques and lessons of your youth and may have to revisit the early days again. But, you are older and things change as you age. What should you do to regain and possibly improve your playing? This is the question.

Step One

Read the chapters before this and see if some of those sections can help. However, there are some things you should stress more than others, and other things that could be holding you back. The following sections will give you some more ideas for improving.

Hold a Steady Tone

First, make sure you can hold a centered, steady tone, with a beautiful, relaxed quality. Try not to use any vibrato and keep the volume constant. As you age this becomes more and more important. If you find that you can't hold a steady tone, make sure that there is not an underlying health issue. It is possible that you may feel that you are running out of air too soon and your tone starts shaking regardless of how hard you try to hold it steady. This could be a sign of serious health issues. Get checked out! I had this problem and found out that I needed a couple of stents. After they took care of me, the problem resolved and my strength and air support returned.

Don't Rush the The Return

You may remember, rightly or wrongly, how well you played at certain times in your life and want to regain those great playing days of yesteryear. The danger is trying to get those times back too quickly, and you hurt yourself or get discouraged. For starters, forget about the wonder years and just try to get a beautiful, steady tone. From the beautiful, steady tone, start to expand by playing easy tunes at around an mf or where you find your best tone to be. You don't want to sound pinched by playing too softly or harshly, and un-centered by playing too loudly. Just relax. Take your time and make beautiful music. Don't worry about playing high or having chops of steel. By the way, mf means mezzo-forte, not Maynard Ferguson.

Expand

From this starting point you can gradually expand in all directions as long as you can keep the beautiful, steady tone. This slow, gradual recovery is the fastest way to get to a point where playing becomes satisfying. Also, you might think about changing your expectations throughout this journey. At the time of this writing, I am 73 and enjoying playing more than I ever have. I might actually be doing some things better since I have the time to practice things I never had time for when I was playing full time. Then, I was going from piece to piece, style to style, and just trying to survive. Now is the time to enjoy and take care of any unfinished business.

Too Many Approaches

Hopefully this book can take you to the next level, but try not to get confused by trying too many approaches at the same time. It's as bad as trying to use all the theories of the golf swing at the same time. As Gary Player said "Paralysis Through Analysis". I would change it to "Over Analysis". There are so many great teaching methods and systems that it is important that you find the right one for you. At first, avoid the extremes. Later on, it's possible that the extreme could be just what you need.

Most of all, enjoy, have fun, and keep a good attitude on your next journey.

Lou Cucunato, Glen Quarrie, Bill Helmers, and Dennis Najoom playing at a local coffee house.

"Respecting others is one of the most important aspects of being a good human"

—Dennis Najoom

Chapter 17

Thoughts, Notes , and Tips

"Respecting others is one of the most important aspects of being a good human."

Listen to the great players.

Be inspired by them, then make your playing your own.

Practice all the scales and scale variations.

Not just major, minor, pure, melodic and harmonic. Be sure to do whole tone, diminished, half diminished, blues, pentatonic, minor pentatonic, bebop, all the modes and all the chord qualities of arpeggios and anything else I've missed.

See Appendix IV for some helpful pentatonic exercises.

Practice the etudes from *Technical Studies for the Cornet* by H L Clark.

Practice them but also vary the chromatics. Exercise one in Clark goes a tri-tone up and a tri-tone down. That's excellent and cool but don't get stuck just doing this and one octave up and down. Try going chromatically up a Major 3rd and down a Major 3rd gradually getting faster and faster, then work on going up and down chromatically any interval; Minor 3rd, Major 2nd, Major 5th and so on and so on.

Make orchestral excerpts part of your practice.

They are great exercises. You'll be learning great music as well as getting some good work on transposition. Get the entire part if you can.

Teachers

When you are studying with a teacher, the teacher should be there for you, and not you there for the teacher and the teacher's needs. Follow your instincts. If you feel something is not quite right trust yourself and do what is necessary. Change schools if you're in college or just find a teacher more suited for you. The teacher may be wonderful but not right for you. Do what you have to do.

The problem with some teachers is they teach the students their own problems and how to correct them.

Some teachers can be bullies as well and will try to shape you into an exact copy of themselves. Run! Don't fall into their web.

Especially be careful of the charismatic self-appointed musical Guru, or any self-appointed Guru for that matter. They feed off of you, their loyal students. They should never demand loyalty. Run, but remain respectful of course. Your loyalty is earned and granted to them, if deserved.

Take control of your education.

Ultimately you are your own teacher. In other words, *take the bull by the horns.*

Play for musicians other than trumpet players.

Play for musicians you respect other than trumpet players. They won't take into account problems inherent to trumpet playing.

Help your musical colleagues.

Help your musical colleagues whenever possible. We're all in this together. Build them up and don't try to knock them down. We all have our strengths and weaknesses. Nobody has it all.

Respecting others is one of the most important aspects of being a good human. Respect.

Most importantly, take care of yourself.

Eat right, exercise, rest and try to keep a good attitude. These things are not always easy in the music business. But, remember that you are making music and creating the ability to enhance people's lives. It is a very worthy endeavor. There is great joy in seeing a person smile when you play.

Make good friends, enjoy, and cherish your time as a musician.

Dennis Najoom

Appendices

Appendix I

Mouthpiece 1

Dennis Najoom

Start at a comfortable *mf* and vary the dynamics as you warm up.

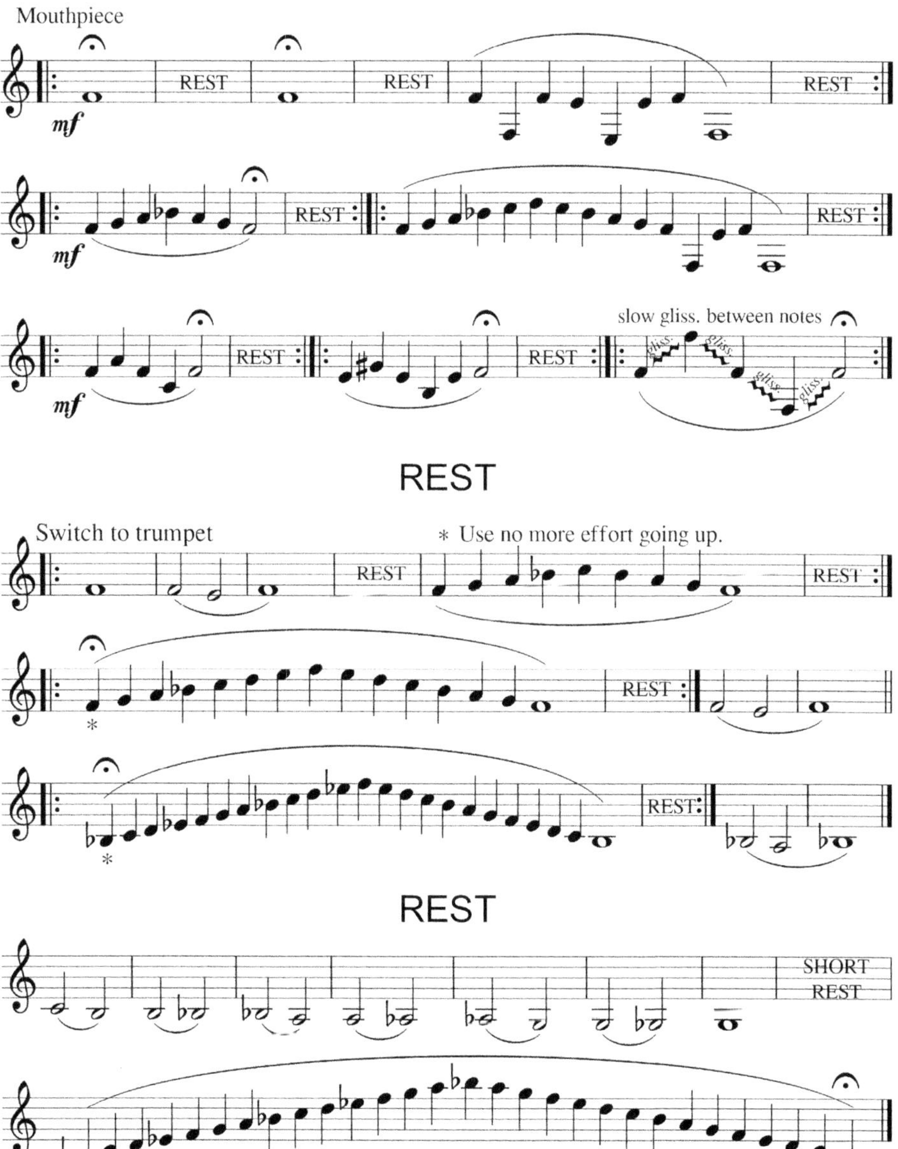

Notes:

Mouthpiece 2

Dennis Najoom

1. Repeat as Needed 2. Rest as Needed

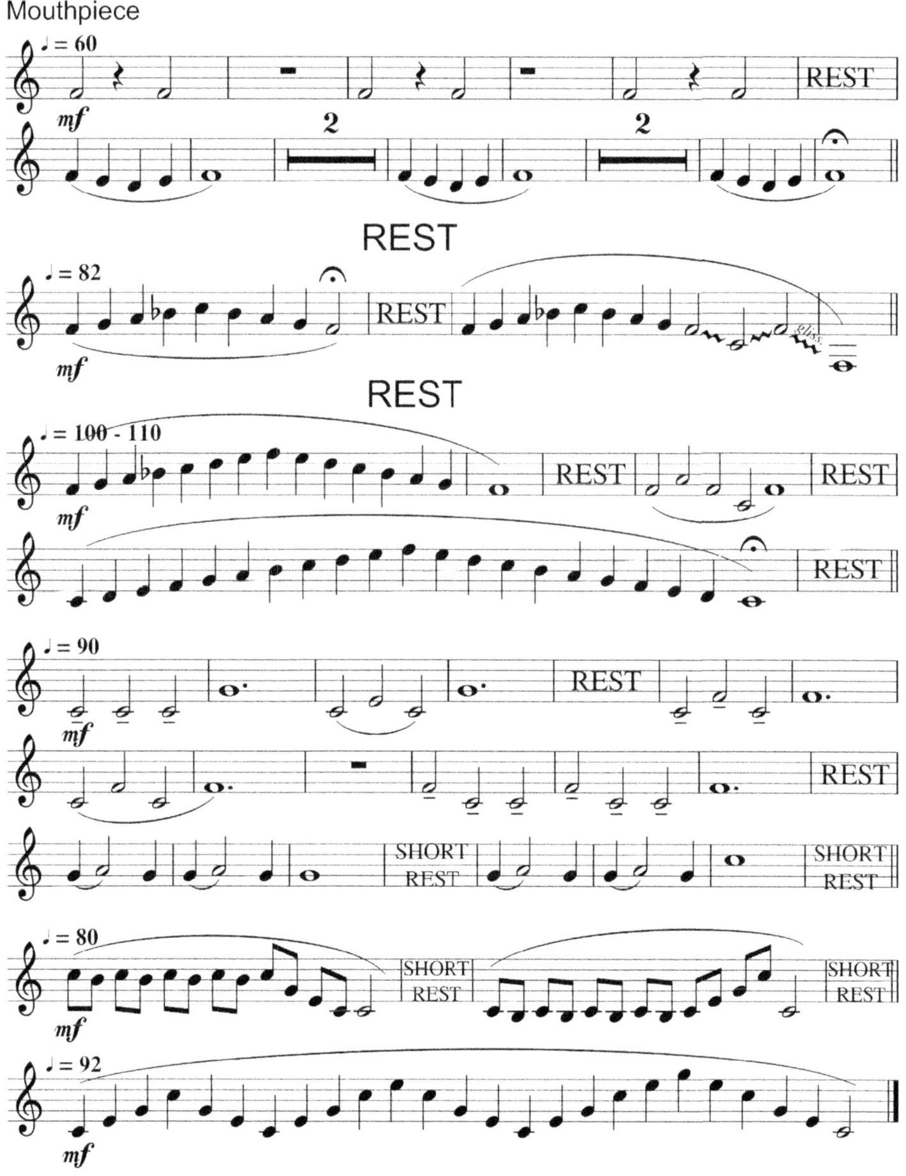

Notes:

Appendix II

Sensitivity 1
For Trumpet

Dennis Najoom

Feel the Resistance

When doing this exercise:

1. **Use no more effort going up** and
2. **Mirror effort going down**

As you go up, allow the increased resistance to let you get softer. Reopen as you go down and get louder to where you began as resistance lessens.

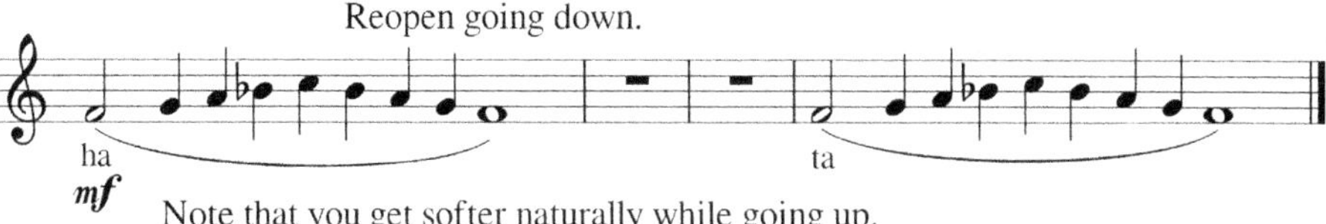

REST before going on.

Notes:

Sensitivity 2

For Trumpet

Dennis Najoom

Feel the Resistance

Sensitivity II uses the same notes as Sensitivity I, however this time:

1. Meet the same resistance going up by blowing harder.
2. It's okay if your volume increases while going up.

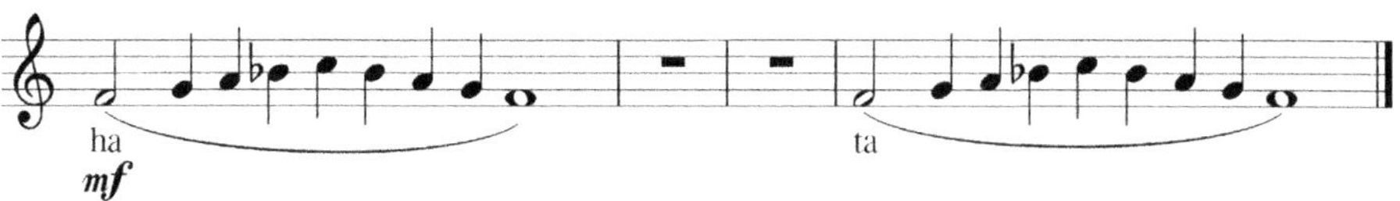

REST before going on.

Notes:

Appendix III

3 Ways to Play

For Trumpet

When playing musical lines, think about the 3 ways to play, and incorporate them as you play each phrase. As time goes on this can become natural.

Way #1

In #1 you will find that in order to play with a beautiful tone and good intonation, your aperture will slightly go from more open to more closed.

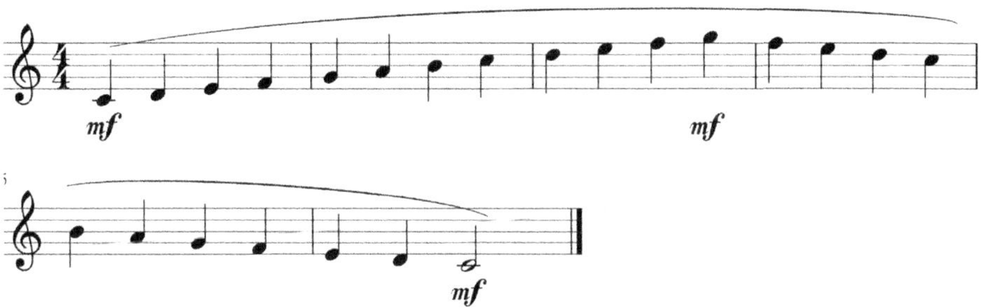

Way #2

In #2 the change of aperture from low to high will be much more pronounced from big to small.

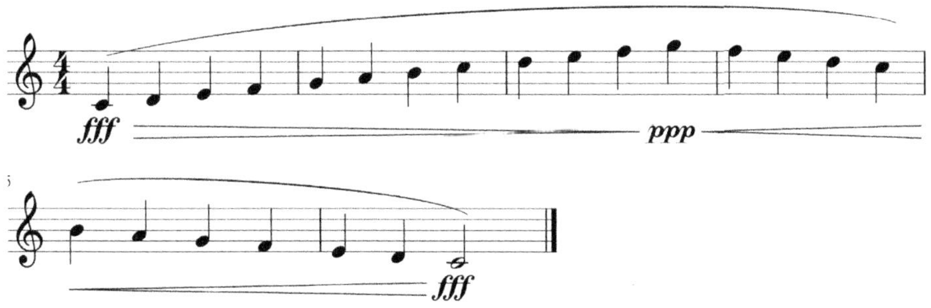

Way #3

In #3, if done to extreme, will be the only time the aperture can remain the same.

These three exercises will train you to play the following exercise. I find this training exercise a lot of fun (and very hard).

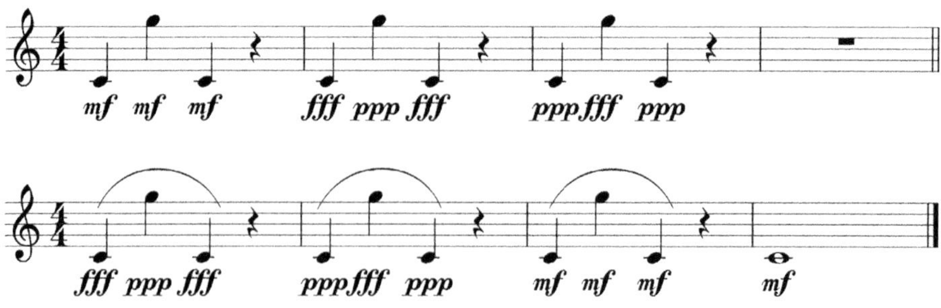

Appendix IV

Pentatonics

Attention: This is <u>not</u> a theory lesson.

There are different ways to think about the theory of pentatonics, but one approach is to hear and internalize these sounds. Try to learn and internalize the many different scales and progressions to the same degree of proficiency that you already know the diatonic major scale. Thinking too hard can slow and stymie the creative response.

Hearing and instinct are good goals. Stimulate your own creativity by making up your own scales and progressions. Get creative. Reading music is only part of the equation.

Take a look at the major pentatonic and minor pentatonic exercises that follow, and have some fun.

Notes:

Appendix IV

Do Some Major Pentatonic

Play these notes in any order with any rhythm. Then, add passing tones and dynamics to make musical lines. Once you are comfortable with this progression:

- Transpose to other keys. *See Chapter 12.*
- Make up your own progressions.
- Make up your own melodies.

Write your own major pentatonic exercises.

Appendix IV

Do Some Minor Pentatonic

Play these notes in any order with any rhythm. Then, add passing tones and dynamics to make musical lines. Once you are comfortable with this progression:

- Transpose to other keys. *See Chapter 12.*
- Make up your own progressions.
- Make up your own melodies.

[Add a flatted 5th and you have a blues scale.]

Write your own minor pentatonic exercises.

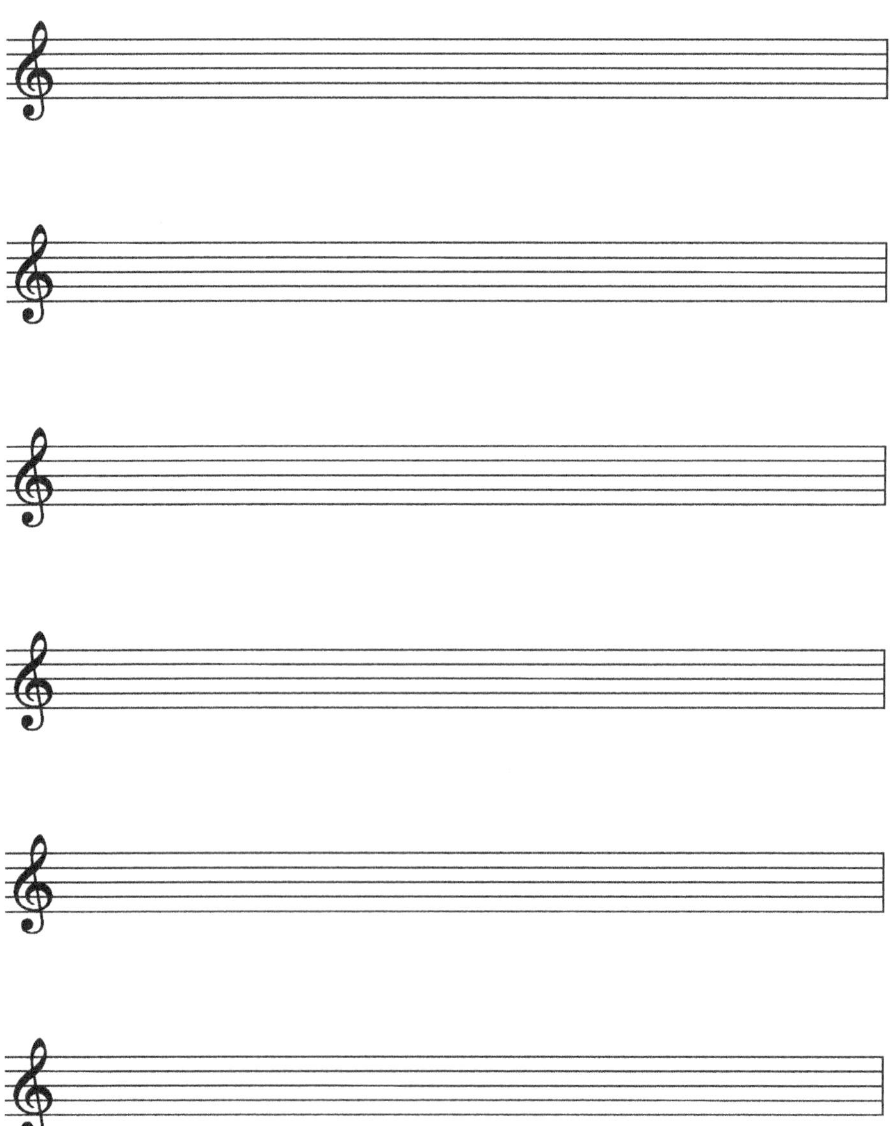

Appendix V

Low Note Warm up

Dennis Najoom

lip bend = Slight jaw drop will open the embouchure to achieve a ½ step lower, maintaining the previous fingering.

Appendix V

Write your own low note warm up

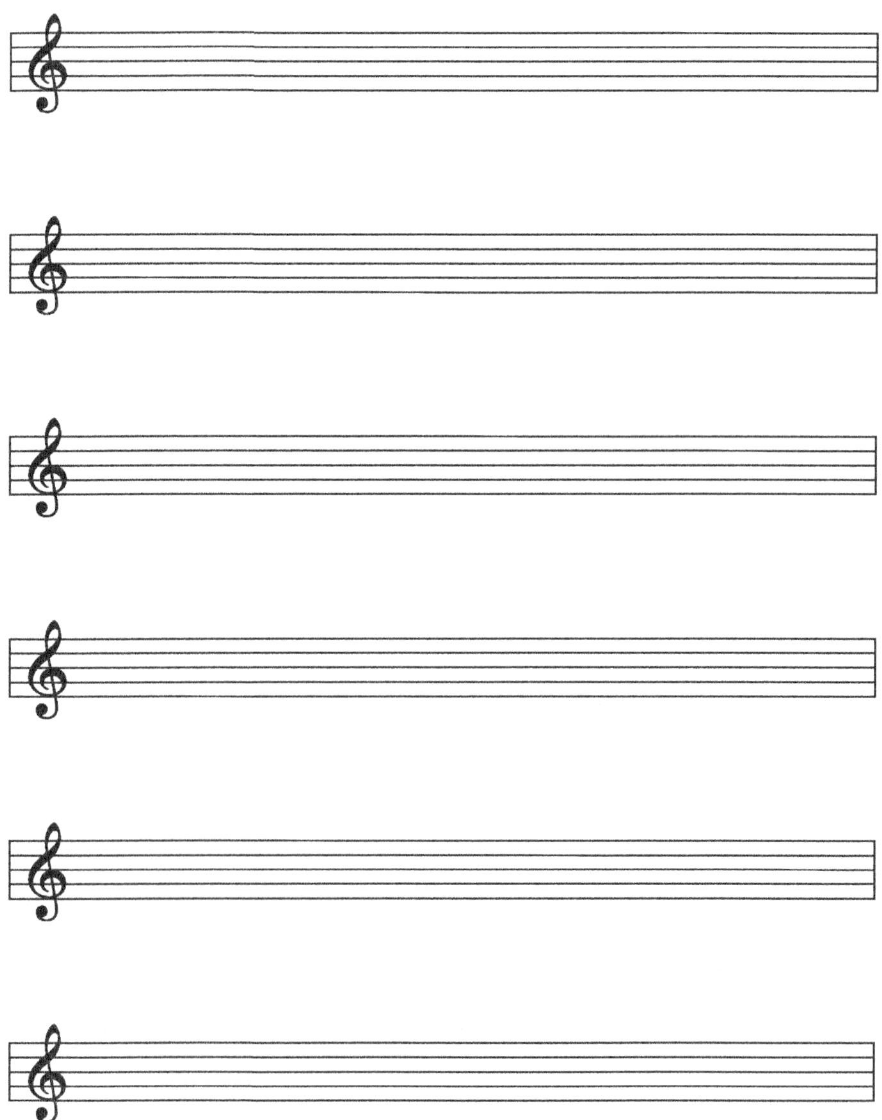

Chord Quality Etude

Dennis Najoom

lip bend = Slight jaw drop will open the embouchure to achieve a ½ step lower, maintaining the previous fingering.

Appendix V

Write your own etude

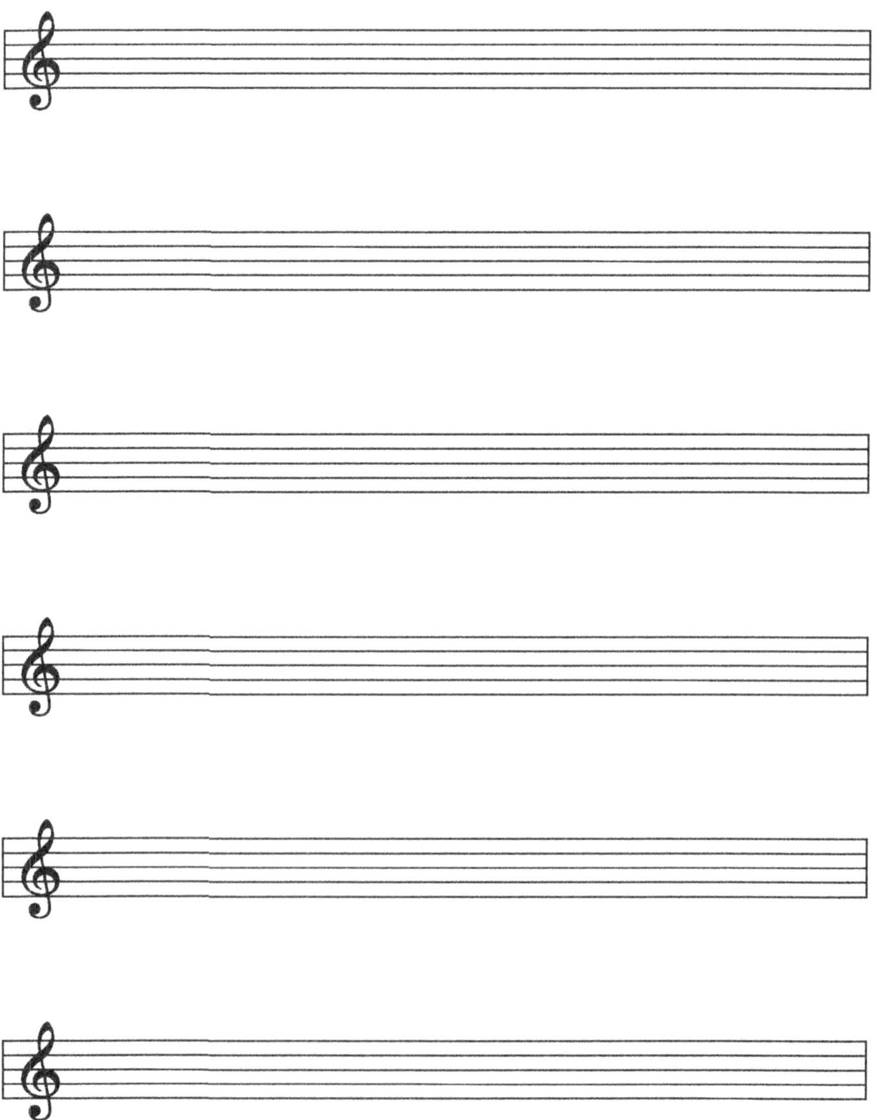

Just Some Simple Things

Dennis Najoom

Appendix V

Write your own music!

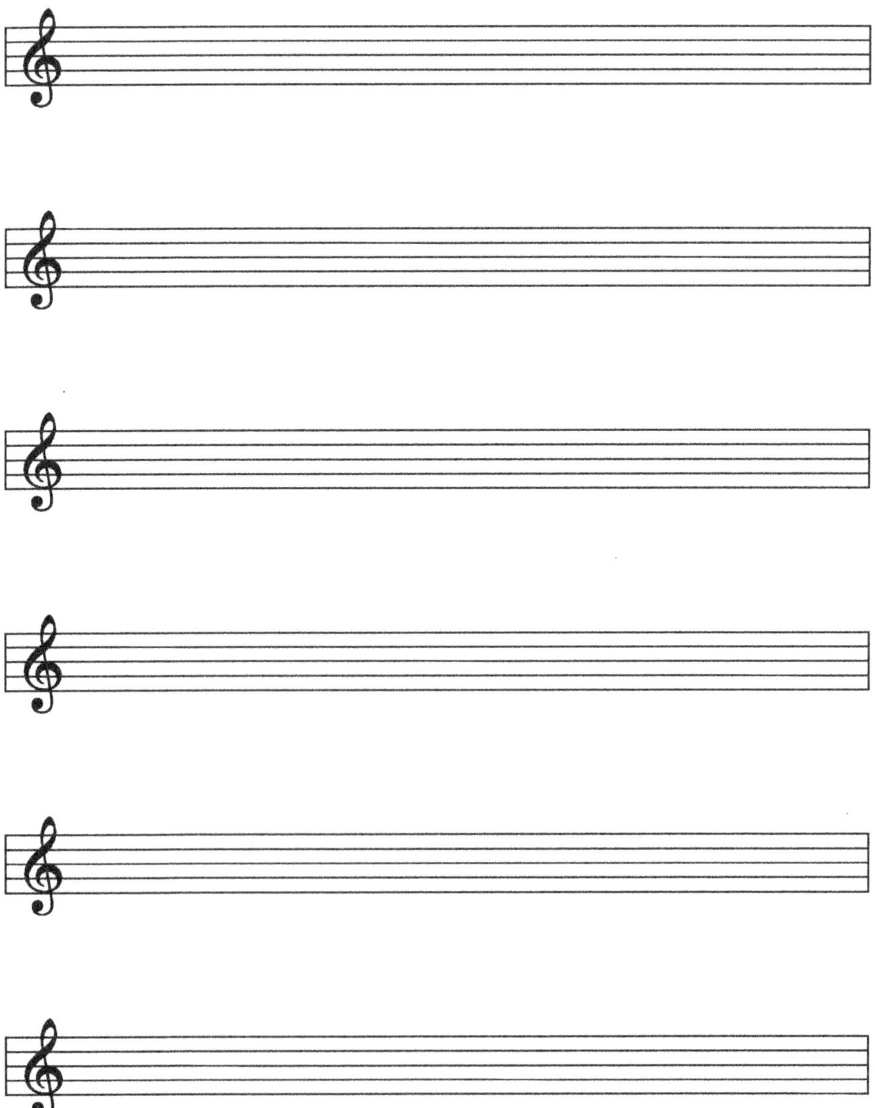

Dennis Najoom grew up in Pittsfield, Massachusetts, and studied trumpet with his uncle George Fulginiti until it was time to go to The Hartt College of Music. At Hartt, his trumpet teachers were Ronald Kutik, Robert Nagel, and Roger Murtha. Other teachers include Roger Voisin, Armando Ghitalla, Seymour Rosenfeld, Mel Broiles, Marvin Stamm, and Arnold Jacobs.

In 1967 and 1968 Najoom was a fellow at the Tanglewood Music Festival. He played with the Hartford Symphony Orchestra for five years until joining the Milwaukee Symphony Orchestra for 43 years. In the MSO, the titles he held longest were Co-principal and Pops Principal, and he was also a frequent soloist.

He has performed with the Philadelphia Orchestra and still performs with the MSO occasionally. In 2015 he formed a seven piece traditional jazz band, the Little Lake Stompers, which performs frequently in a local club and does educational concerts for the Milwaukee Symphony ACE program. Najoom is also known for Najoom Music Products leadpipes and mouthpieces.

Printed in Great Britain
by Amazon

FLOR.

A terrific guide for all serious trumpet players and musicians in all genres. Najoom offers insights on musicianship, and real life tips and tricks from his own experiences as a professional trumpet player.

It includes;
- A chapter on transposing along with a chart to carry in your instrument case.
- A chapter on Pops playing for the orchestral musician.
- A chapter for the older and comeback player.
- Najoom's own exercises for warming up and gaining sensitivity.

and many other important but easy to understand techniques for all musicians.

A practical, concise, and entertaining handbook for all levels and generations.

"I love it. *Trumpet According to Dennis Najoom*, is the best book about trumpet ever. I wish I wrote it." —Mario Guarneri, L.A. Philharmonic, L.A. studio trumpet, Inventor of the "Berp"

"*Trumpet According to Dennis Najoom*, is a great new book essential for every trumpeter's library. I have known Dennis for over 30 years, and no one else in the business combines Dennis' trumpet virtuosity, thoughtful teaching, and extensive experience with instrument and mouthpiece design, all of which are reflected in his new book. He writes about essential topics rarely mentioned in trumpet books, including aperture control, how to think about equipment, orchestral Pops performance, and perhaps most importantly, how to be a good colleague and have a successful long term career. Everyone from student to pro will gain from Dennis' knowledge and experience."

—John Urness, Principal Trumpet Orquesta Sinfónica del Estado de México

Cover Photography & Design by Jennifer Najoom

ISBN 9781735997902
9 781735 997902
90000